NUMBERS
IN GOD'S WORLD

written by
Beverly Beckmann

illustrated by
Jules Edler

CONCORDIA®

Publishing House
St. Louis

Copyright © 1983 Concordia Publishing House
3558 S. Jefferson Avenue, St. Louis, MO 63118
Manufactured in the United States of America

3 4 5 6 7 8 9 10 11 DP 89 88 87 86 85 84

D1377916

In God's world only one leaf was left
on the maple tree.

High in the tree it clung to the small twig.

2

In God's world two squirrels scampered to collect nuts.

Up in the tree was their warm hiding place.

3

In God's world three turtles slowly plodded
toward the pond.

Down in the water they would be warm.

In God's world four kittens hurried down the path.

Under the barn floor mother cat was waiting.

5

In God's world five snowflakes
were blown by the wind.

Down, down, down they floated to the cold ground.

6

In God's world six children built a snowman.

Up on the top they placed the old beat-up hat.

In God's world seven twigs lay on the ground.

Next to each other some looked small
and some looked big.

8

In God's world eight weeds
grew between the sidewalk cracks.

Up to the sunlight they popped.

In God's world nine ants formed a straight line.

In front of them was a picnic basket.

10

In God's world ten carrots waited to be pulled.

Beneath the ground grew the fat orange vegetable.

In God's world many things can be touched, smelled, tasted, seen, and heard.

1 Leaf

2 Squirrels

3 Turtles

4 Kittens

5 Snowflak

Find them and count them.

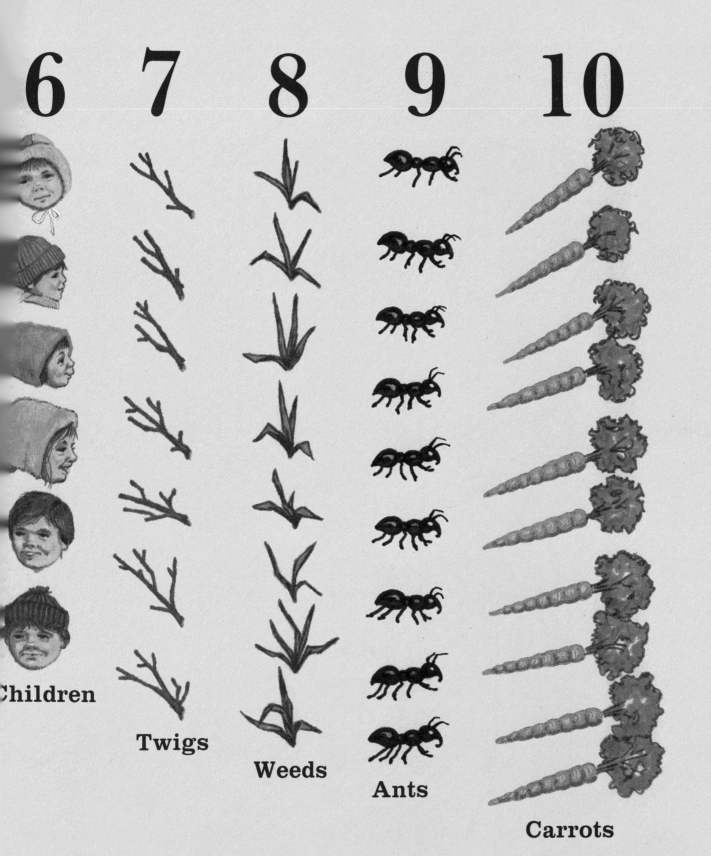

6   7   8   9   10

Children   **Twigs**   **Weeds**   **Ants**   **Carrots**

Dear Family Members,

This book was written to introduce your child to math symbols and also to help you reinforce the concept behind the symbol.

Rote counting is like reciting a nursery rhyme. The numerical order is important, but a good parent wants the child to understand the concept behind it, too. To do this, here are some suggestions: Have the child place his or her finger on the objects as they are counted. Even more important, take the child on a walk and look for the objects in God's creation. As the child touches and feels the objects, have him or her count them.

Working and playing together, you and your child can develop a foundation for later mathematical skills. But even more can be developed through this experience. The child will feel the order in God's universe. God had a plan as He created. The numerical sequence reinforces this plan of orderliness.

Enjoy with your child the orderliness of God's creation and the joy of touching and feeling His craftsmanship.

Beverly Beckmann

Beverly Beckmann